**Mel Bay Presents**

# Easy Classics for VIOLA

With Piano Accompaniment

Piano Accompaniments by **Jannette Spitzer** and **Laura Spitzer**

Selected and Arranged by **Peter Spitzer**

AF120084

The *Easy Classics* books were written to provide beginning to intermediate students with an enjoyable introduction to some of the greatest classical melodies.

The violin, viola, and cello books are fully compatible, and may be played in any combination, with or without piano accompaniment. (Note to the pianist: Solo and duet parts are shown in the upper staff, in treble clef. Depending on the instrument, actual pitch may be in a lower octave.)

Easy Classics books for violin, viola, and cello are presented in keys suitable for strings, while the books for clarinet, flute, trumpet, and alto saxophone are transposed to keys suitable for wind instruments.

Peter Spitzer

### Include works by:
Beethoven, Tchaikovsky, Mozart, Brahms, Haydn, Schubert, Borodin, Rimsky-Korsakov, Bach, Strauss, Offenbach, Bizet, di Capua, Rossini

1 2 3 4 5 6 7 8 9 0

© 2012 BY MEL BAY PUBLICATIONS, INC., PACIFIC, MO 63069.
ALL RIGHTS RESERVED. INTERNATIONAL COPYRIGHT SECURED. B.M.I. MADE AND PRINTED IN U.S.A.
No part of this publication may be reproduced in whole or in part, or stored in a retrieval system, or transmitted in any form or by any means, electronic, mechanical, photocopy, recording, or otherwise, without written permission of the publisher.

**Visit us on the Web at www.melbay.com — E-mail us at email@melbay.com**

# Contents

| | | Solo/Duet | Piano |
|---|---|---|---|
| Ode to Joy | Beethoven | 4 | 2 |
| Sleeping Beauty Waltz | Tchaikovsky | 6 | 6 |
| Eine Kleine Nachtmusik | Mozart | 8 | 9 |
| Adagio (from Clarinet Concerto) | Mozart | 10 | 12 |
| Hungarian Dance #5 | Brahms | 12 | 14 |
| Emperor Hymn | Haydn | 14 | 16 |
| The Trout | Schubert | 16 | 18 |
| Theme from Polovetsian Dances | Borodin | 17 | 20 |
| Scheherazade | Rimsky-Korsakov | 18 | 22 |
| Jesu, Joy of Man's Desiring | Bach | 19 | 24 |
| Radetzky March | Strauss | 20 | 25 |
| Cancan | Offenbach | 22 | 28 |
| Habanera | Bizet | 24 | 31 |
| Toreador Song | Bizet | 26 | 34 |
| O Sole Mio | di Capua | 28 | 36 |
| William Tell Overture | Rossini | 30 | 38 |

# Ode to Joy
from Symphony #9

Ludwig van Beethoven (1770-1827)

# Sleeping Beauty Waltz
from the ballet "Sleeping Beauty"

Peter Ilich Tchaikovsky (1843-1890)

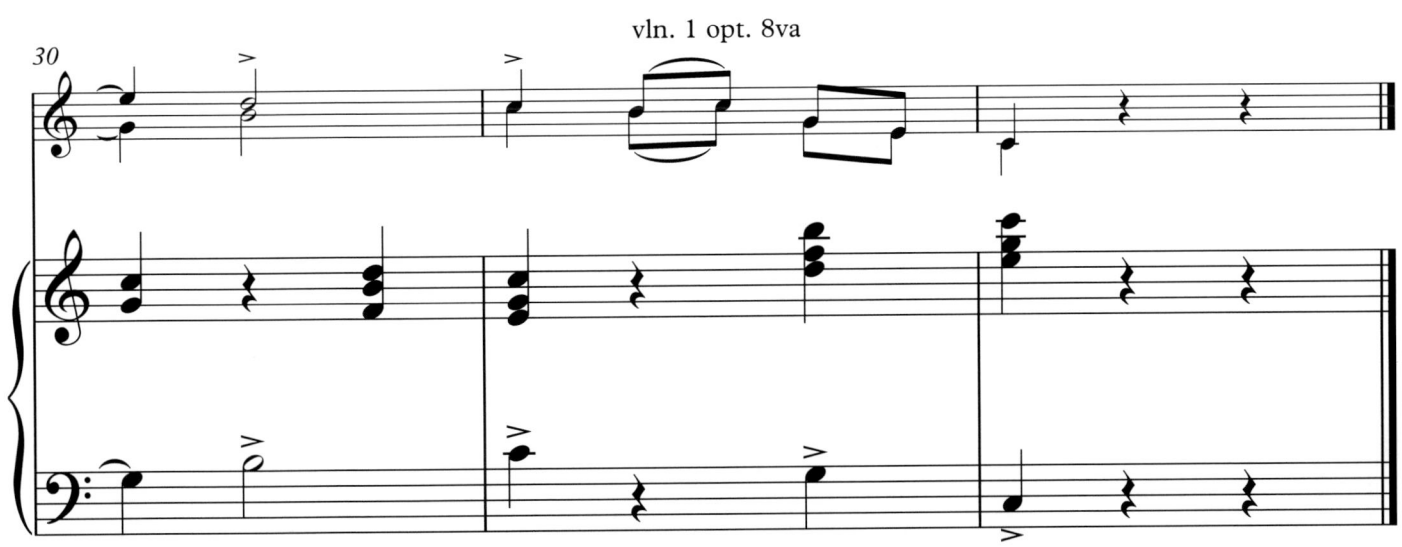

# Eine Kleine Nachtmusik
from Serenade K.525

Wolfgang Amadeus Mozart (1756-1791)

# Adagio
from Clarinet Concerto, K. 622

Wolfgang Amadeus Mozart (1756-1791)

# Hungarian Dance #5

Johannes Brahms (1833-1897)

# Emperor Hymn

Franz Joseph Haydn (1732-1809)

# The Trout

Franz Schubert (1797-1828)

# Theme from Polovetsian Dances
from the opera "Prince Igor"

Alexander Borodin (1833-1887)

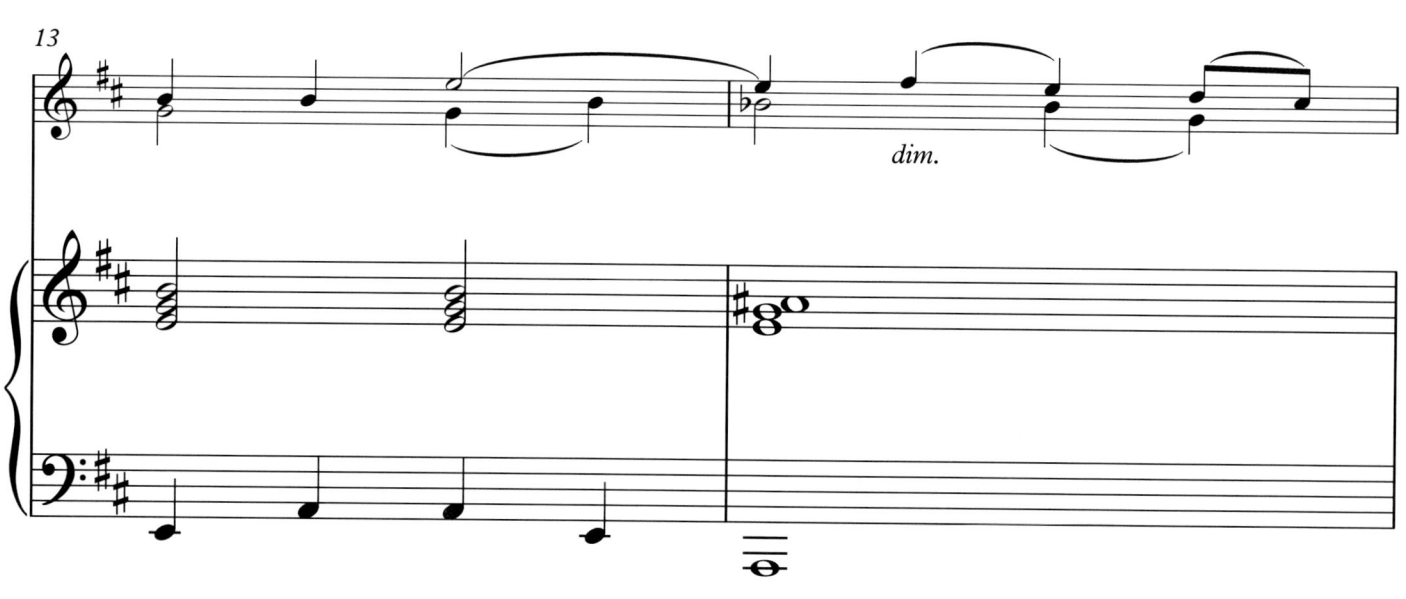

SOLO/DUET

**Include works by:**
Beethoven
Tchaikovsky
Mozart
Brahms
Haydn
Schubert
Borodin
Rimsky-Korsakov
Bach
Strauss
Offenbach
Bizet
di Capua
Rossini

Piano Accompaniments
by **Jannette Spitzer**
and **Laura Spitzer**

Selected and Arranged
by **Peter Spitzer**

1 2 3 4 5 6 7 8 9 0

© 2012 BY MEL BAY PUBLICATIONS, INC., PACIFIC, MO 63069.
ALL RIGHTS RESERVED. INTERNATIONAL COPYRIGHT SECURED. B.M.I. MADE AND PRINTED IN U.S.A.
No part of this publication may be reproduced in whole or in part, or stored in a retrieval system, or transmitted in any form
or by any means, electronic, mechanical, photocopy, recording, or otherwise, without written permission of the publisher.

**Visit us on the Web at www.melbay.com — E-mail us at email@melbay.com**

The *Easy Classics* books were written to provide beginning to intermediate students with an enjoyable introduction to some of the greatest classical melodies.

The violin, viola, and cello books are fully compatible, and may be played in any combination, with or without piano accompaniment. (Note to the pianist: Solo and duet parts are shown in the upper staff, in treble clef. Depending on the instrument, actual pitch may be in a lower octave.)

The *Easy Classics* books for violin, viola, and cello are presented in keys suitable for strings, while the books for clarinet, flute, trumpet, and alto saxophone are transposed to keys suitable for wind instruments.

Special thanks to Mary Helen Weinstein, John Beeman, Judy Roberts, Theresa Frew, Joyce Malick, Carol Masinter, Alan Masinter, Patricia Musgrave, Diana Tucker, and to the many other colleagues and students who helped in developing this series.

Peter

# Contents

| | | Solo/Duet | Piano |
|---|---|---|---|
| Ode to Joy | Beethoven | 4 | 2 |
| Sleeping Beauty Waltz | Tchaikovsky | 6 | 6 |
| Eine Kleine Nachtmusik | Mozart | 8 | 9 |
| Adagio (from Clarinet Concerto) | Mozart | 10 | 12 |
| Hungarian Dance #5 | Brahms | 12 | 14 |
| Emperor Hymn | Haydn | 14 | 16 |
| The Trout | Schubert | 16 | 18 |
| Theme from Polovetsian Dances | Borodin | 17 | 20 |
| Scheherazade | Rimsky-Korsakov | 18 | 22 |
| Jesu, Joy of Man's Desiring | Bach | 19 | 24 |
| Radetzky March | Strauss | 20 | 25 |
| Cancan | Offenbach | 22 | 28 |
| Habanera | Bizet | 24 | 31 |
| Toreador Song | Bizet | 26 | 34 |
| O Sole Mio | di Capua | 28 | 36 |
| William Tell Overture | Rossini | 30 | 38 |

# Ode to Joy
## from Symphony #9

Ludwig van Beethoven (1770-1827)

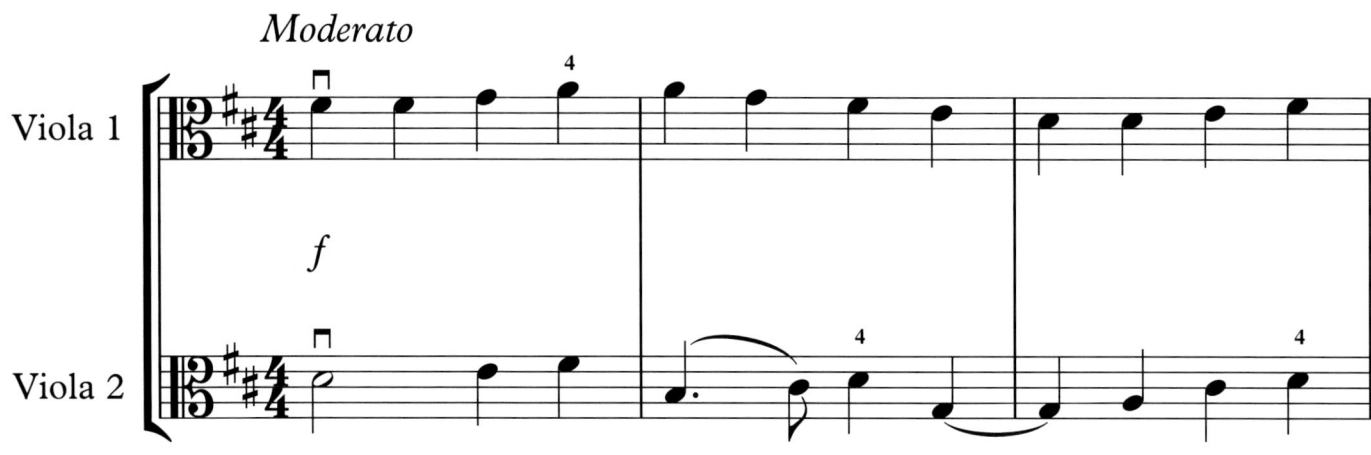

# Sleeping Beauty Waltz
from the ballet "Sleeping Beauty"

Peter Ilich Tchaikovsky (1843-1890)

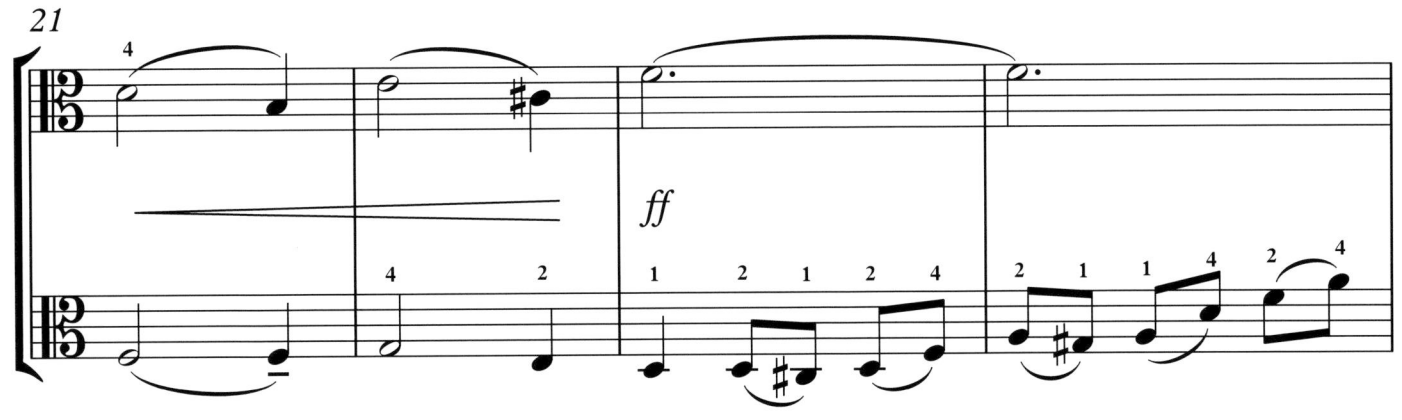
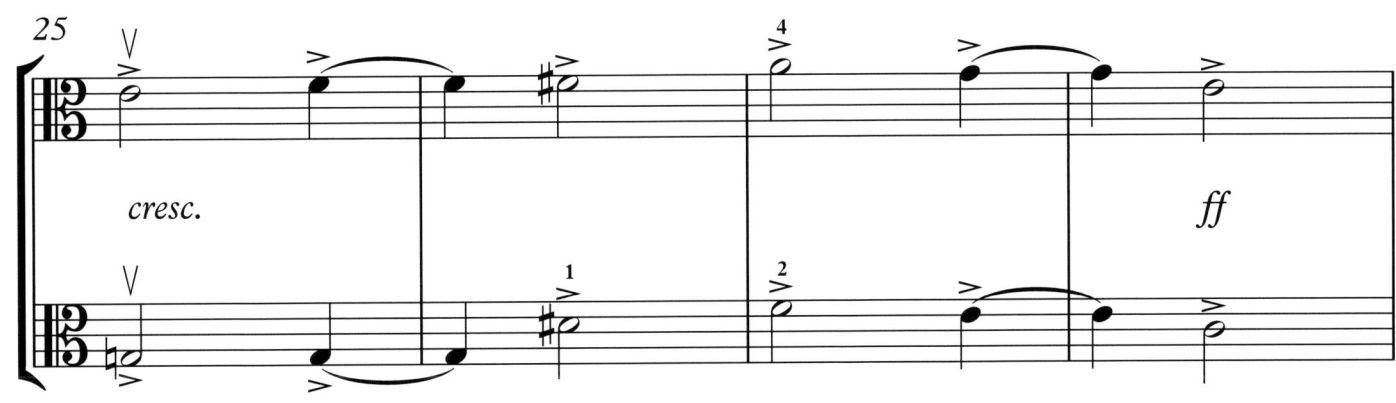
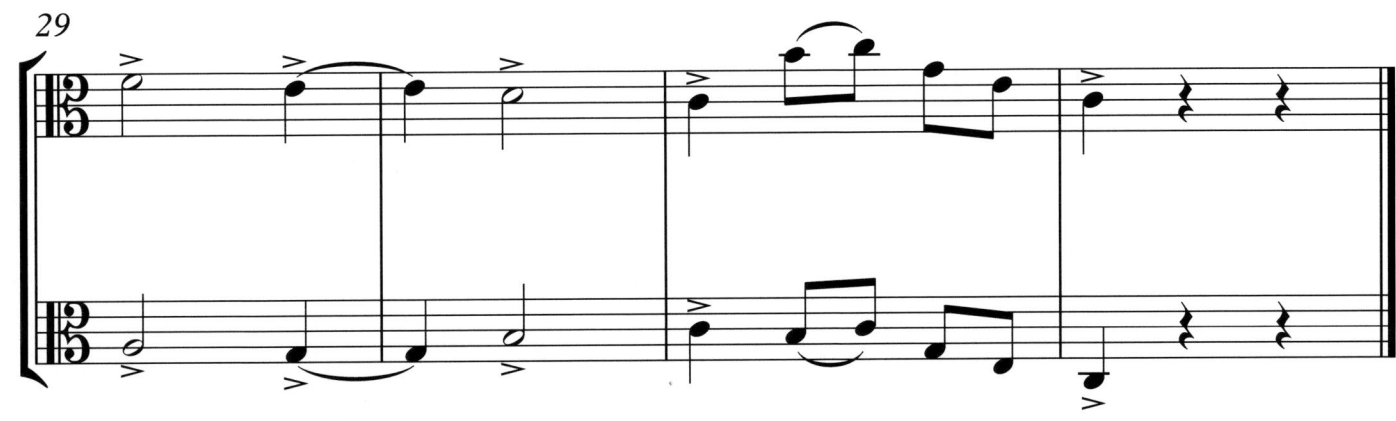

# Eine Kleine Nachtmusik
from Serenade K. 525

Wolfgang Amadeus Mozart (1756-1791)

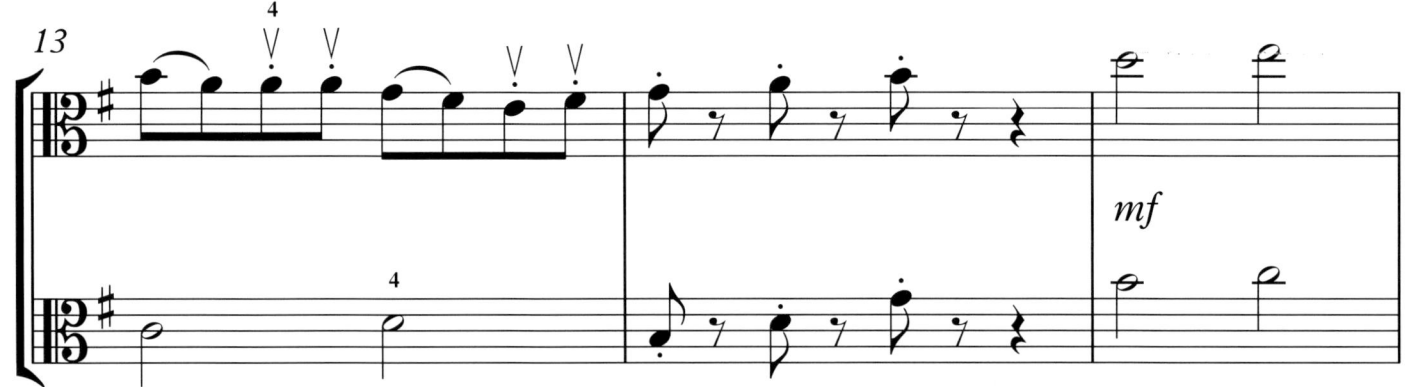
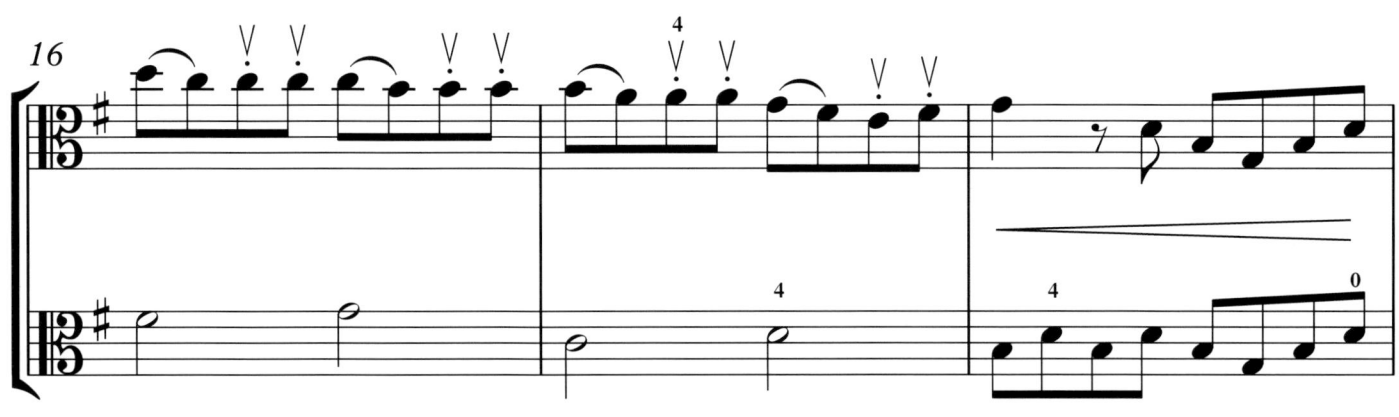

# Adagio
## from Clarinet Concerto, K. 622

Wolfgang Amadeus Mozart (1756-1791)

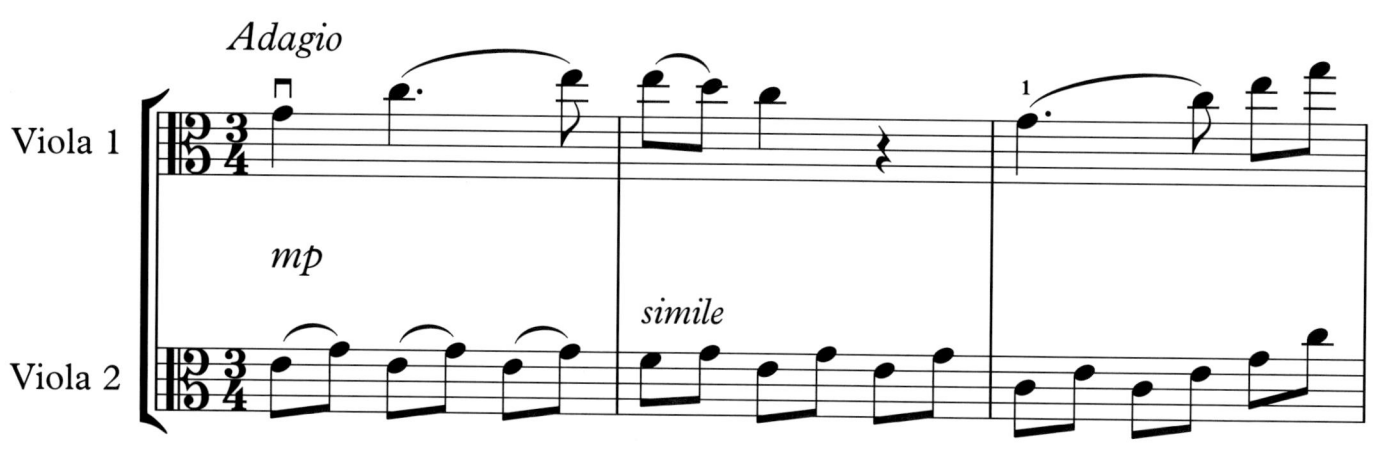

# Hungarian Dance #5

Johannes Brahms (1833-1897)

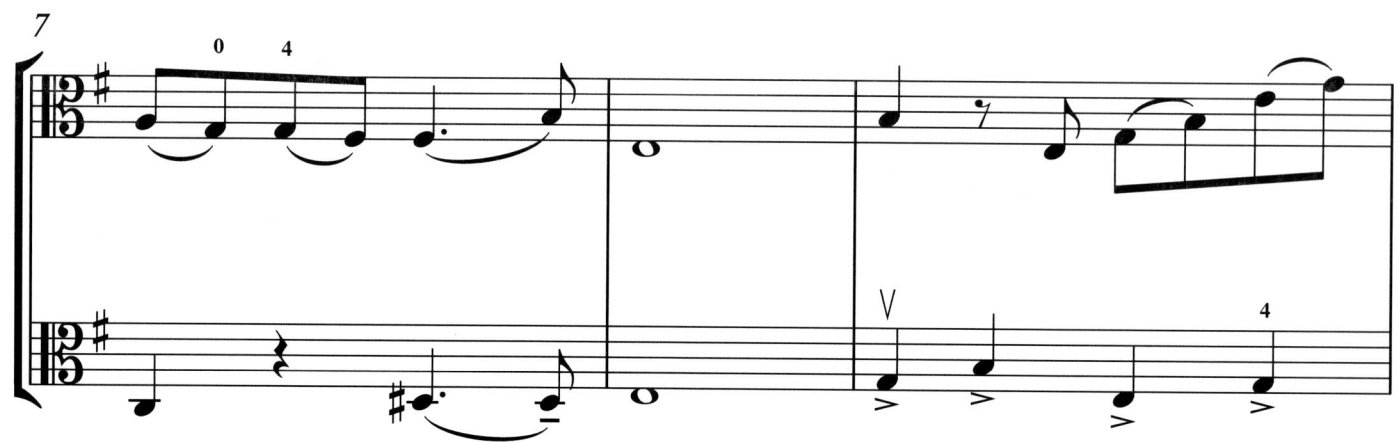

# Emperor Hymn

Franz Joseph Haydn (1732-1809)

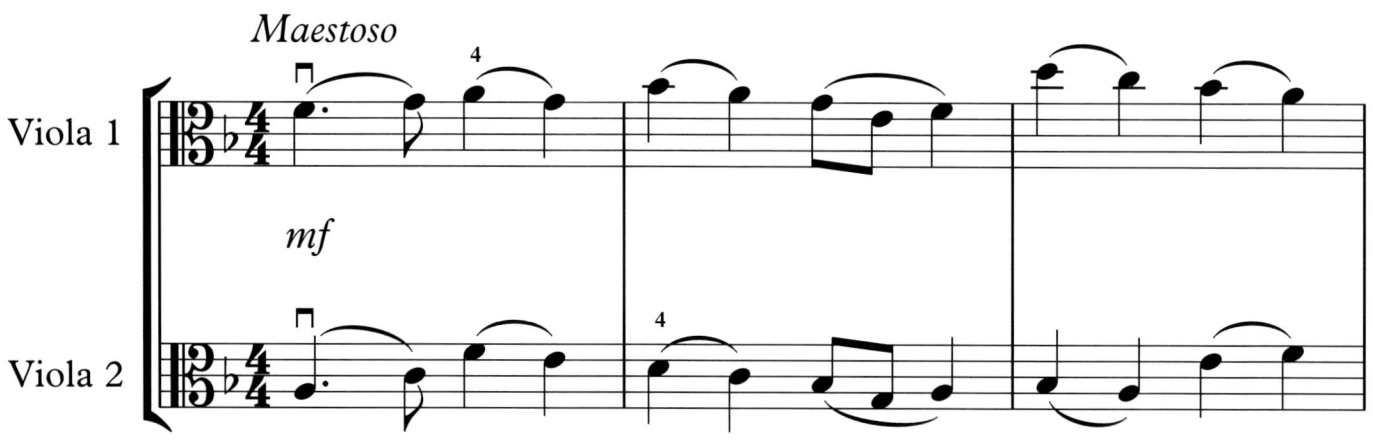
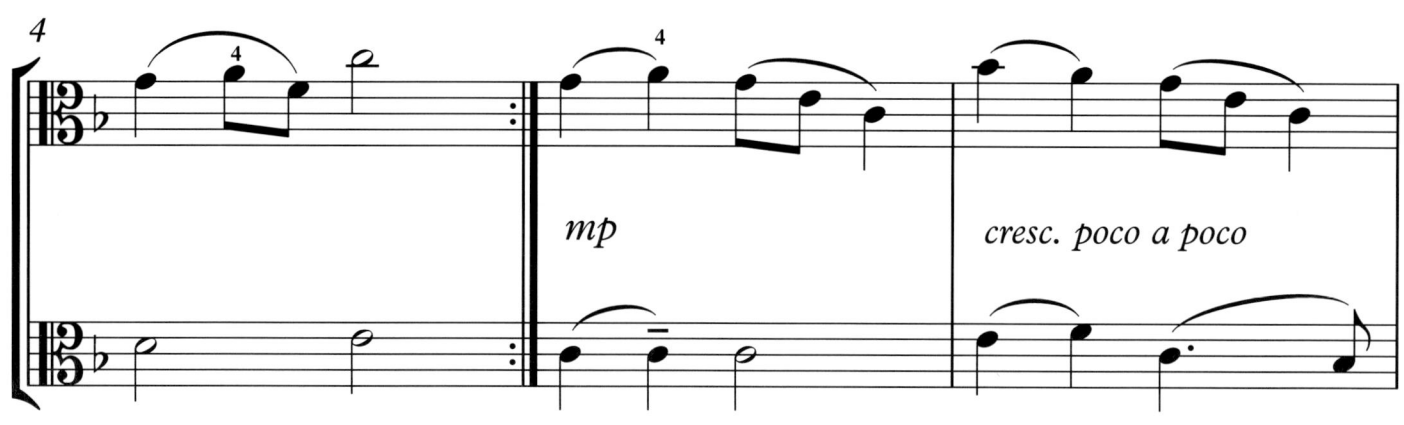

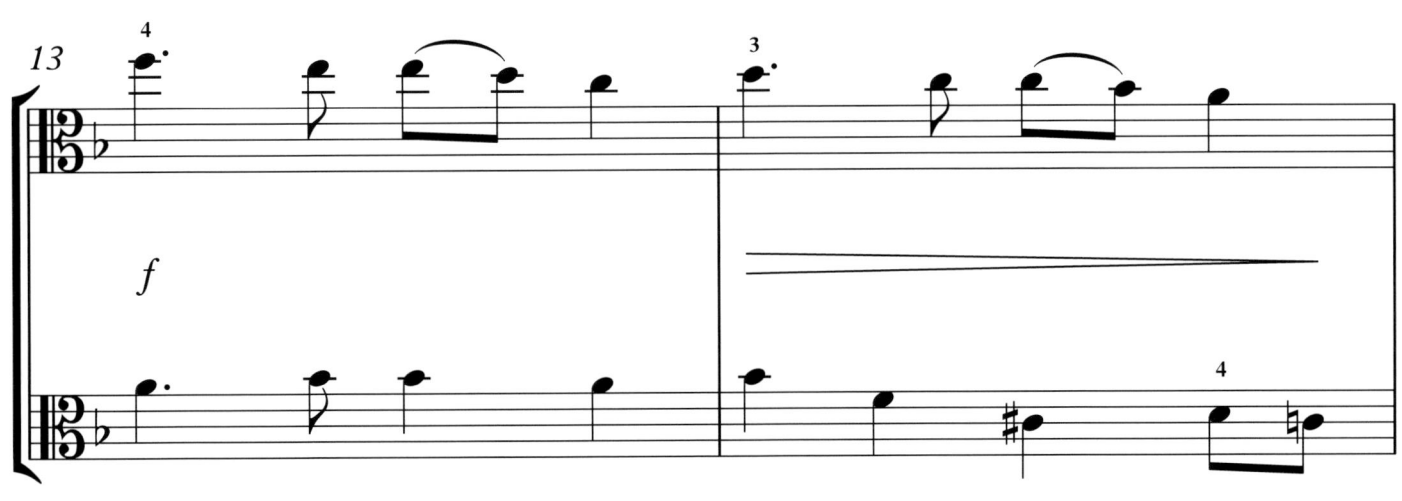

# The Trout

Franz Schubert (1797-1828)

# Theme from Polovetsian Dances
## from the opera "Prince Igor"

Alexander Borodin (1833-1887)

# Scheherazade

Nicholas Rimsky-Korsakov (1844-1908)

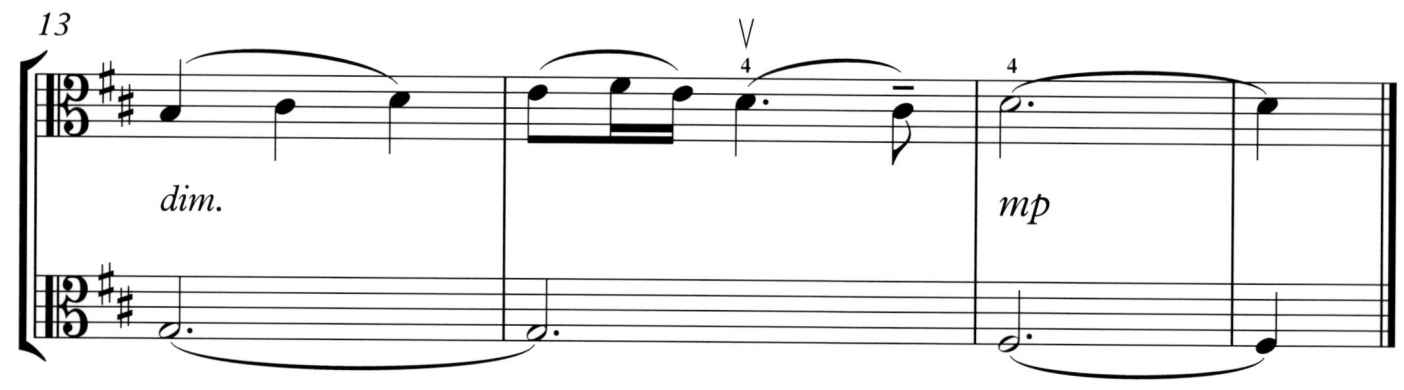

# Jesu, Joy of Man's Desiring
from Cantata No. 147

Johann Sebastian Bach (1685-1750)

# Radetzky March

Johann Strauss (1804-1849)

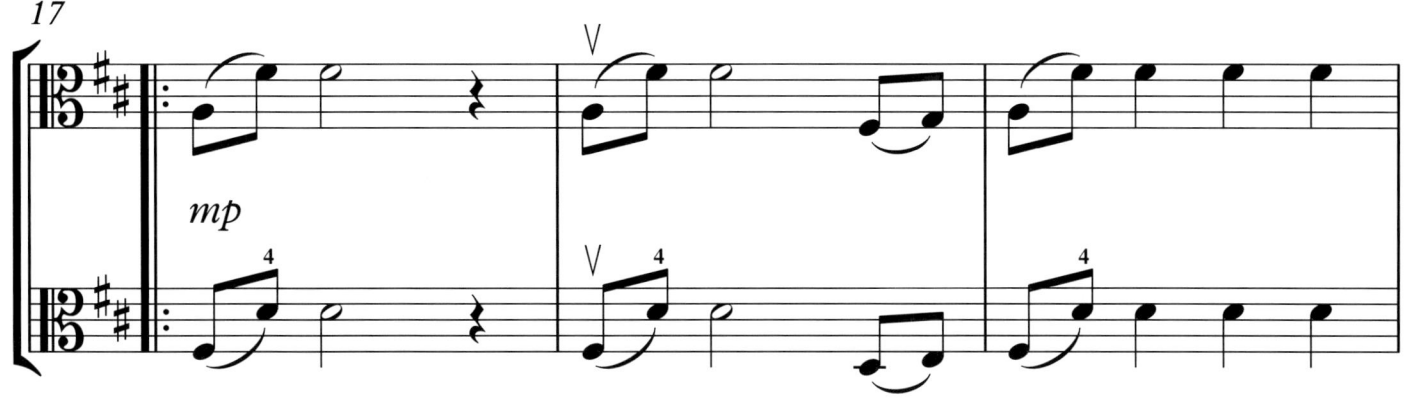

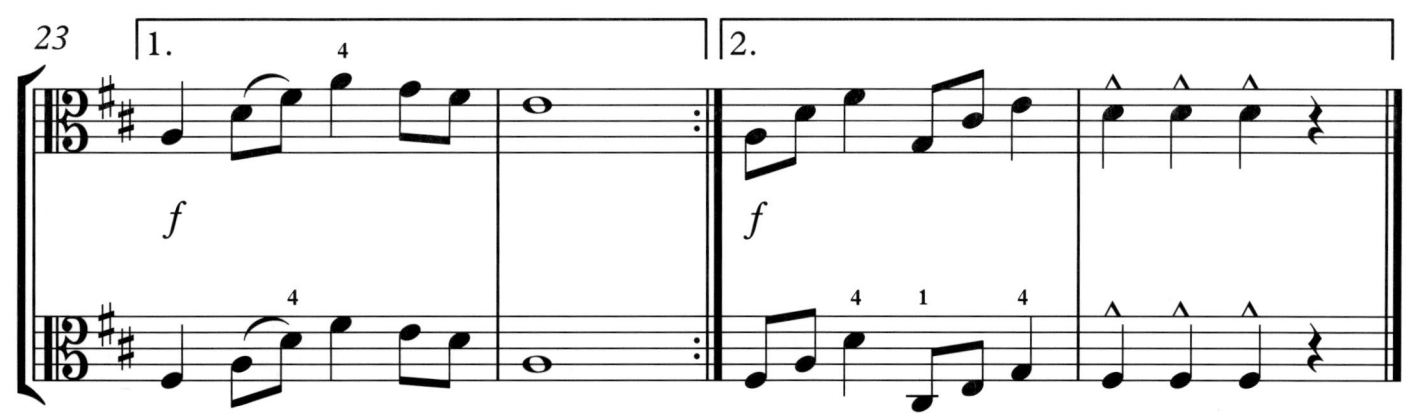

# Cancan
## from the opera "Orpheus in the Underworld"

Jacques Offenbach (1819-1880)

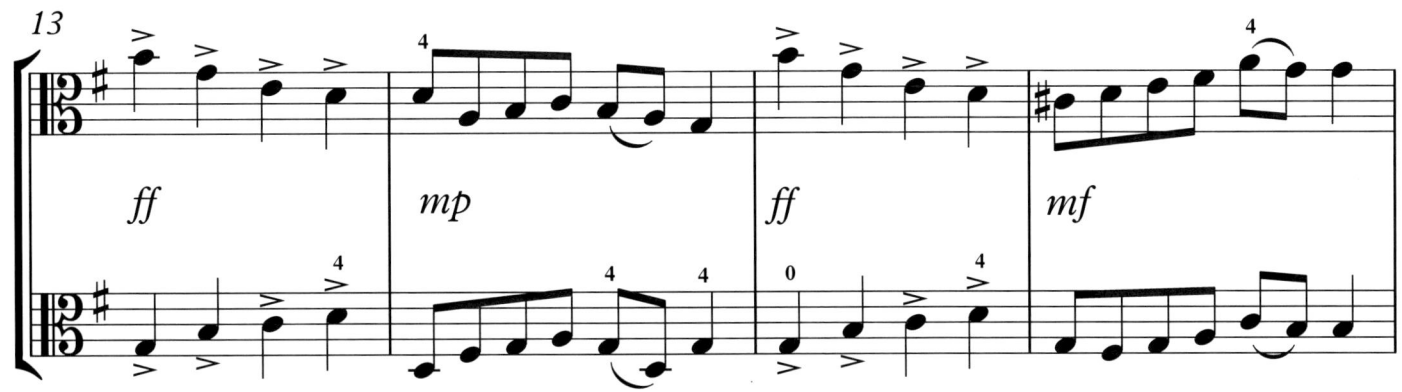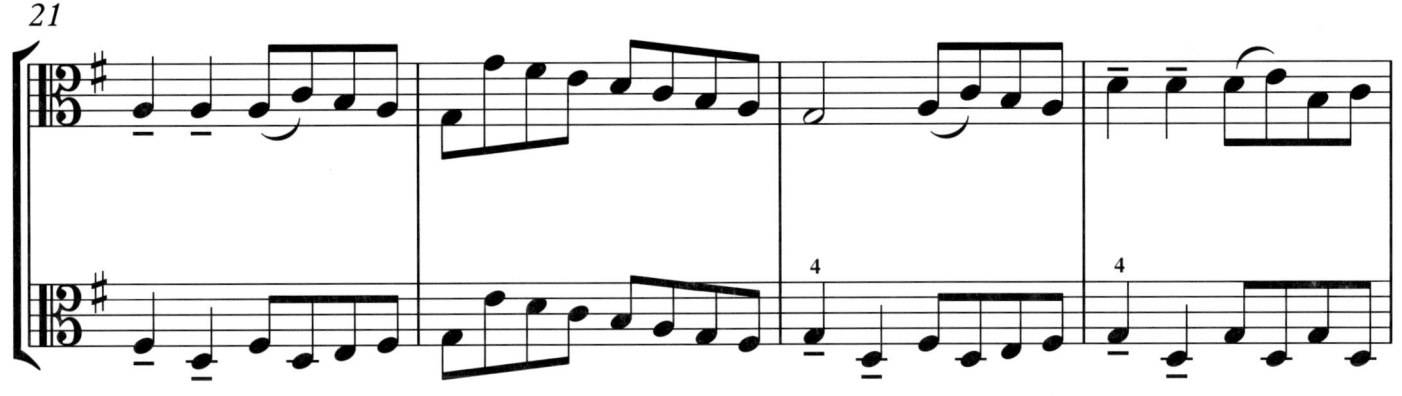

# Habanera
## from the opera "Carmen"

Georges Bizet (1838-1875)

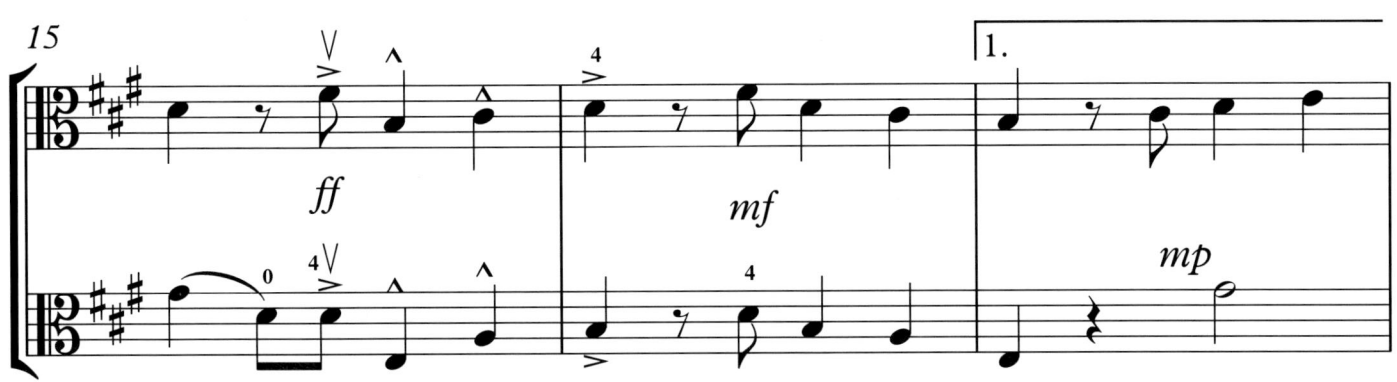

# Toreador Song
## from the opera "Carmen"

Georges Bizet (1838-1875)

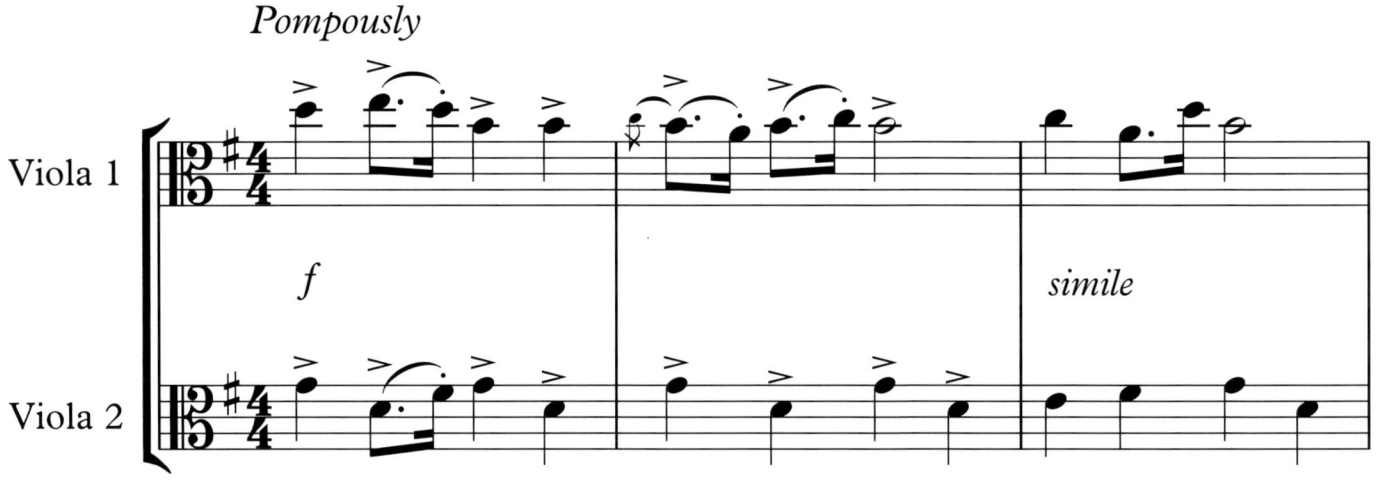

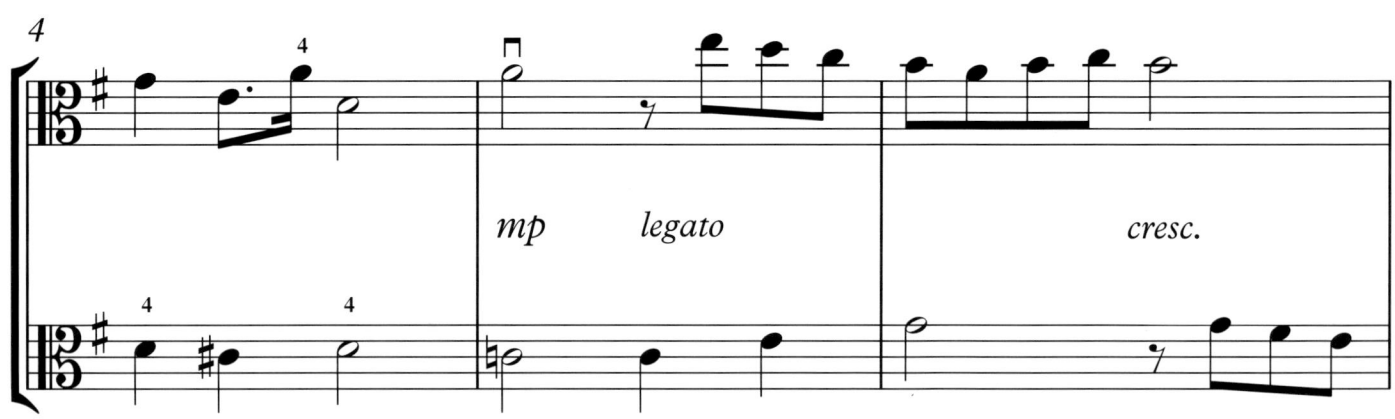

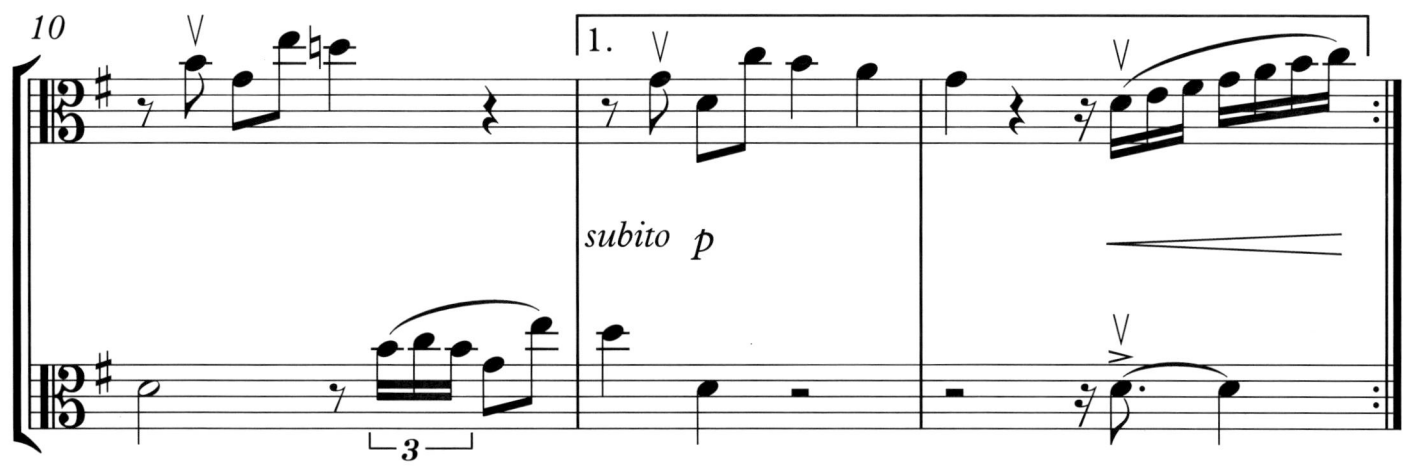
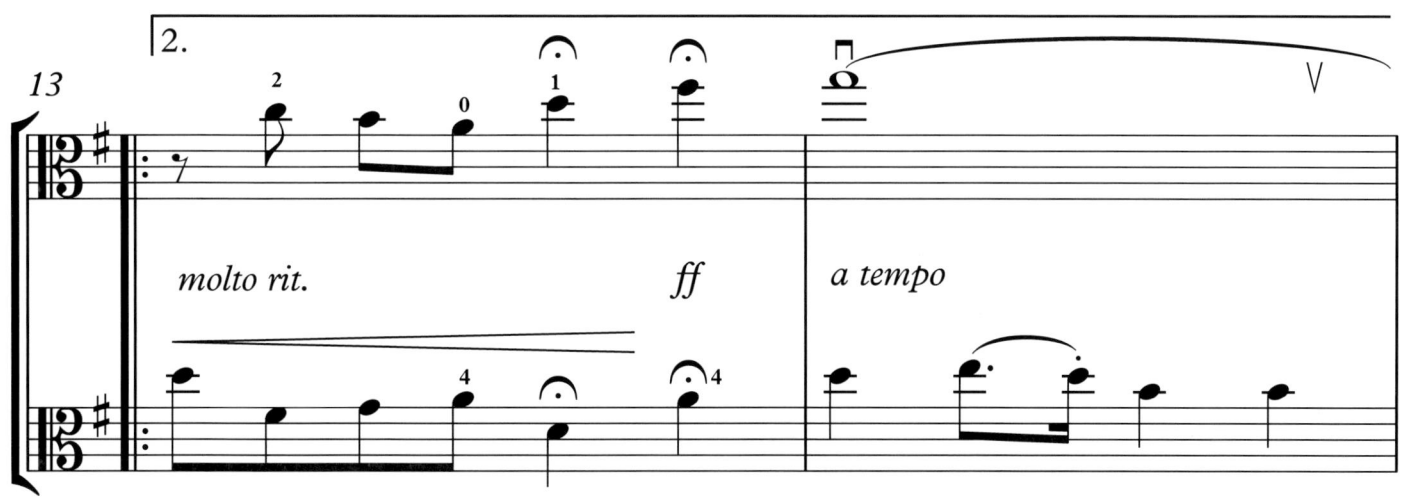
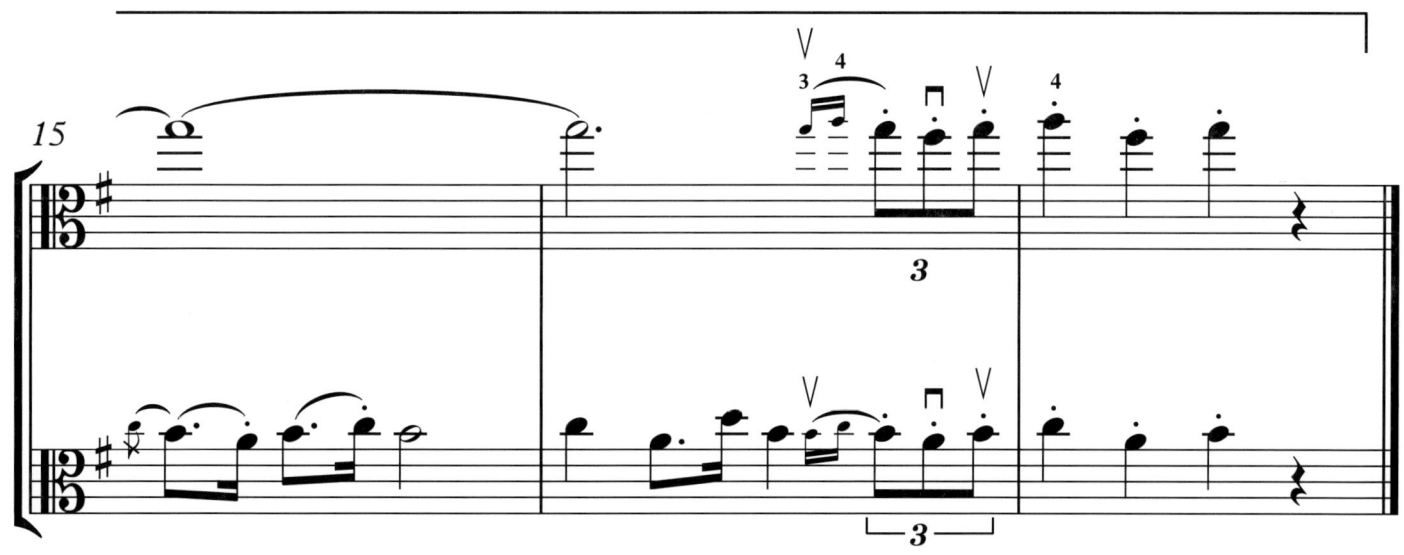

# O Sole Mio

Eduardo di Capua (1864-1917)

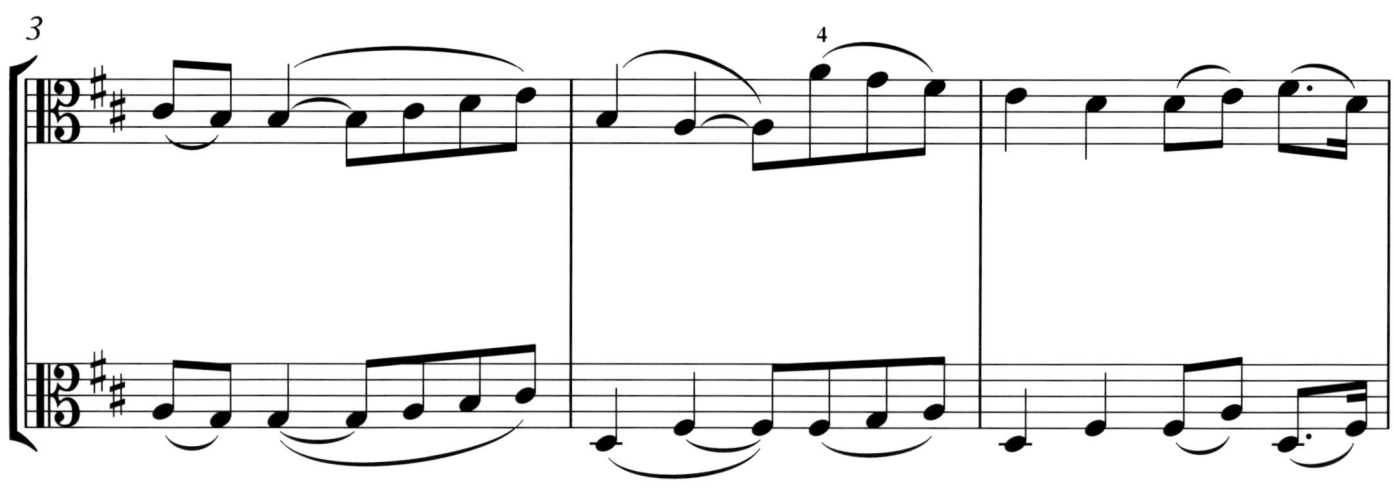

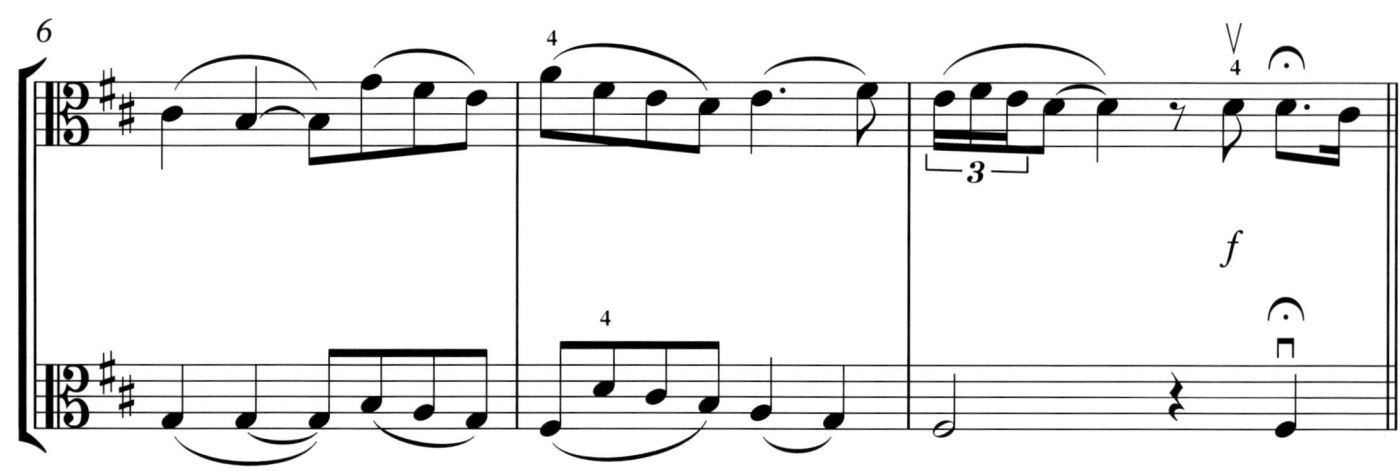

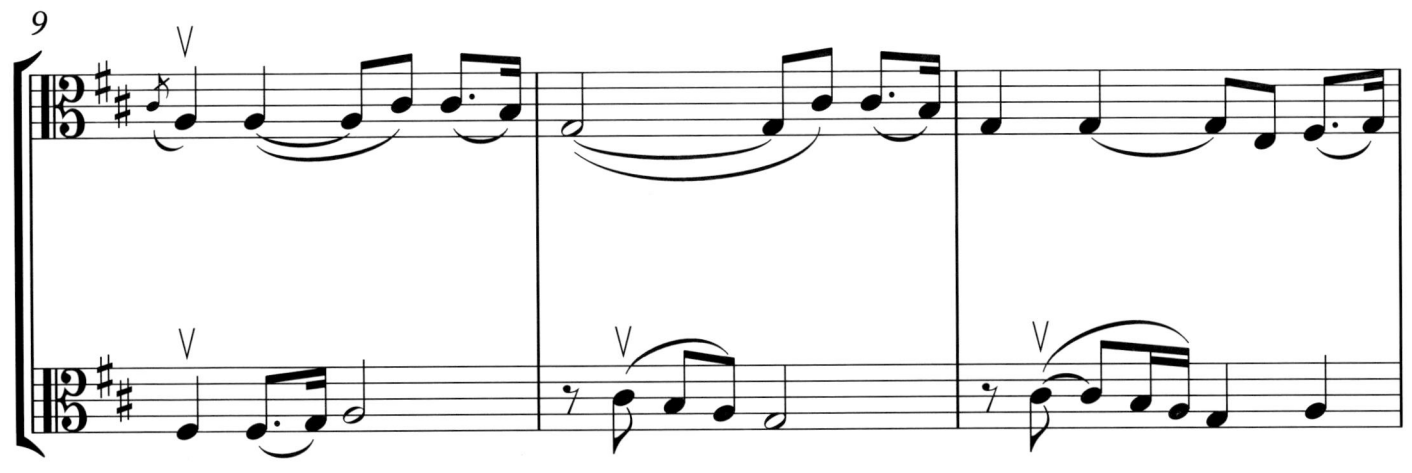

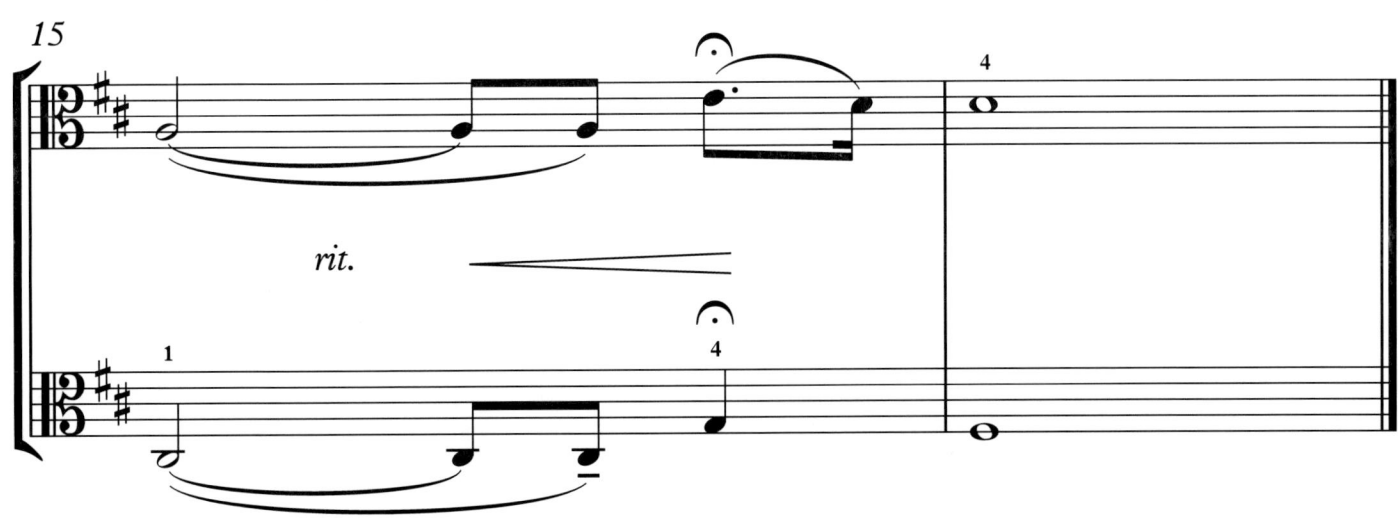

# William Tell Overture
## from the opera "William Tell"

Gioacchino Rossini (1792-1868)

# Scheherezade

Nicholas Rimsky-Korsakov (1844-1908)

# Jesu, Joy of Man's Desiring
from Cantata No. 147

Johann Sebastian Bach (1685-1750)

# Radetzky March

Johann Strauss (1804-1849)

# Cancan

from the Opera "Orpheus in the Underworld"

Jacques Offenbach (1819-1880)

# Habanera
from the opera "Carmen"

Georges Bizet (1838-1875)

31

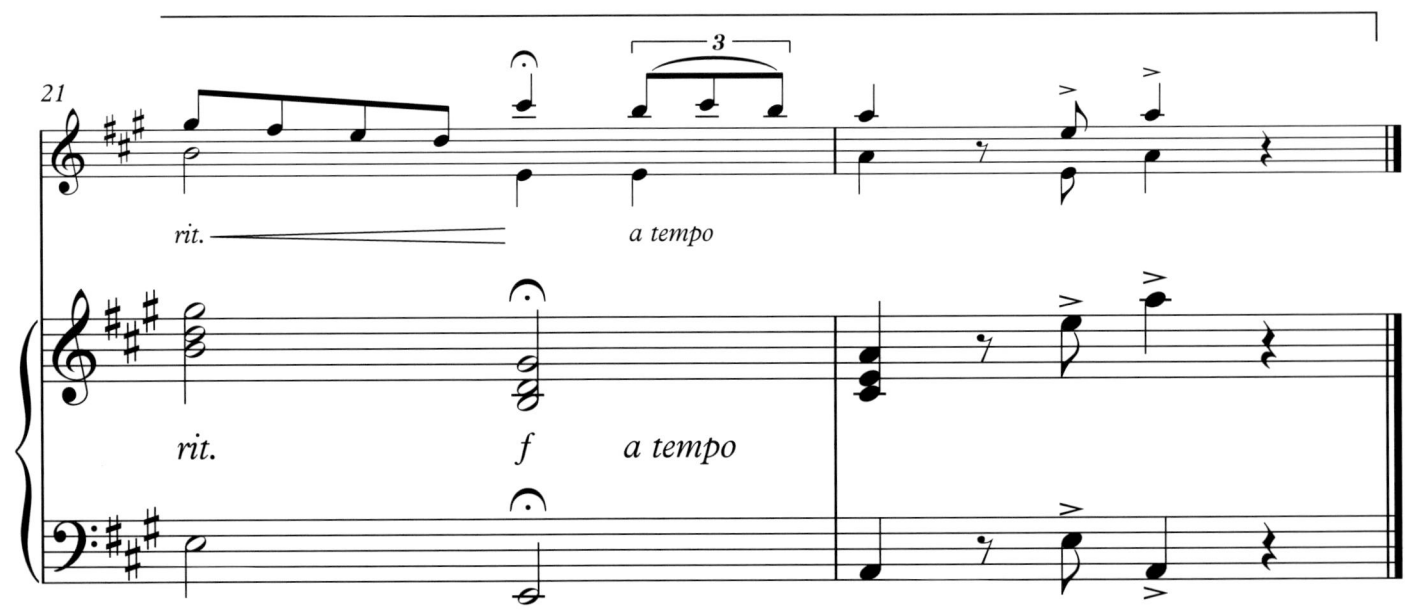

# Toreador Song
from the opera "Carmen"

Georges Bizet (1838-1875)

# O Sole Mio

Eduardo di Capua (1864-1917)

# William Tell Overture
## from the opera "William Tell"

Gioacchino Rossini (1792-1868)

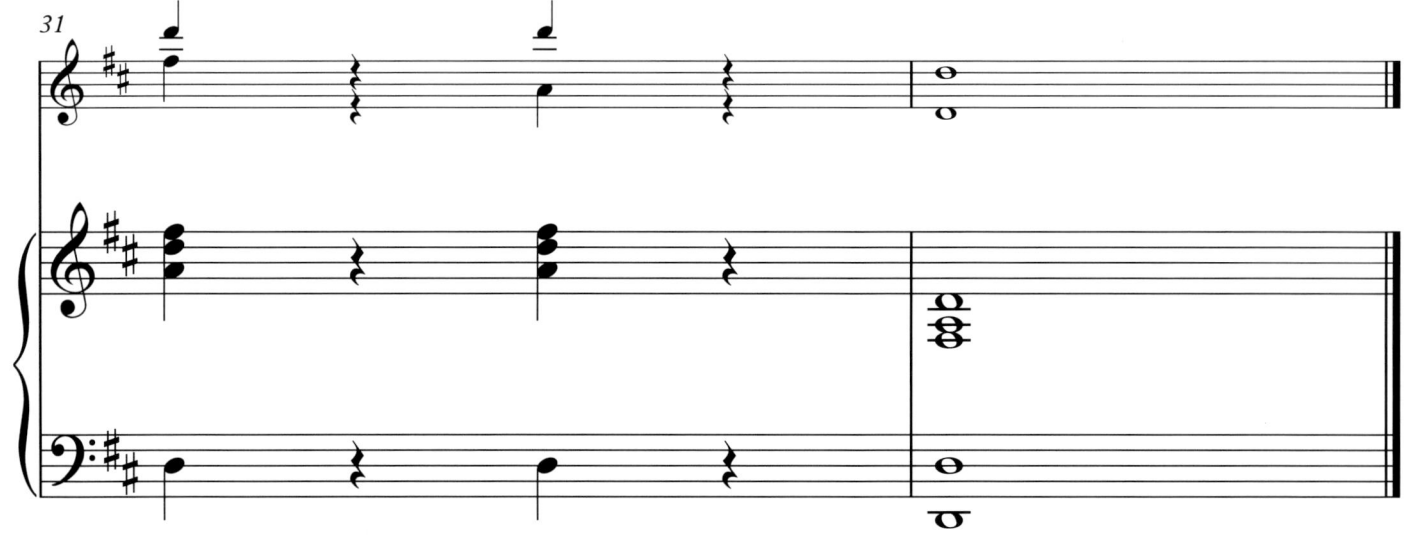